United Synagogue of America
Commission on Jewish Education

NS: One People

written by

Barbara Bar-Nissim

illustrated by

Marlene Lobell Ruthen

Manufactured in the United States of America
ISBN: 0-8381-0719-2

To our children Matthew, Jonathan, Carolyn, Ariella, Russell, and Paula, and to all Jewish children everywhere.

There are Jews living all over the world.

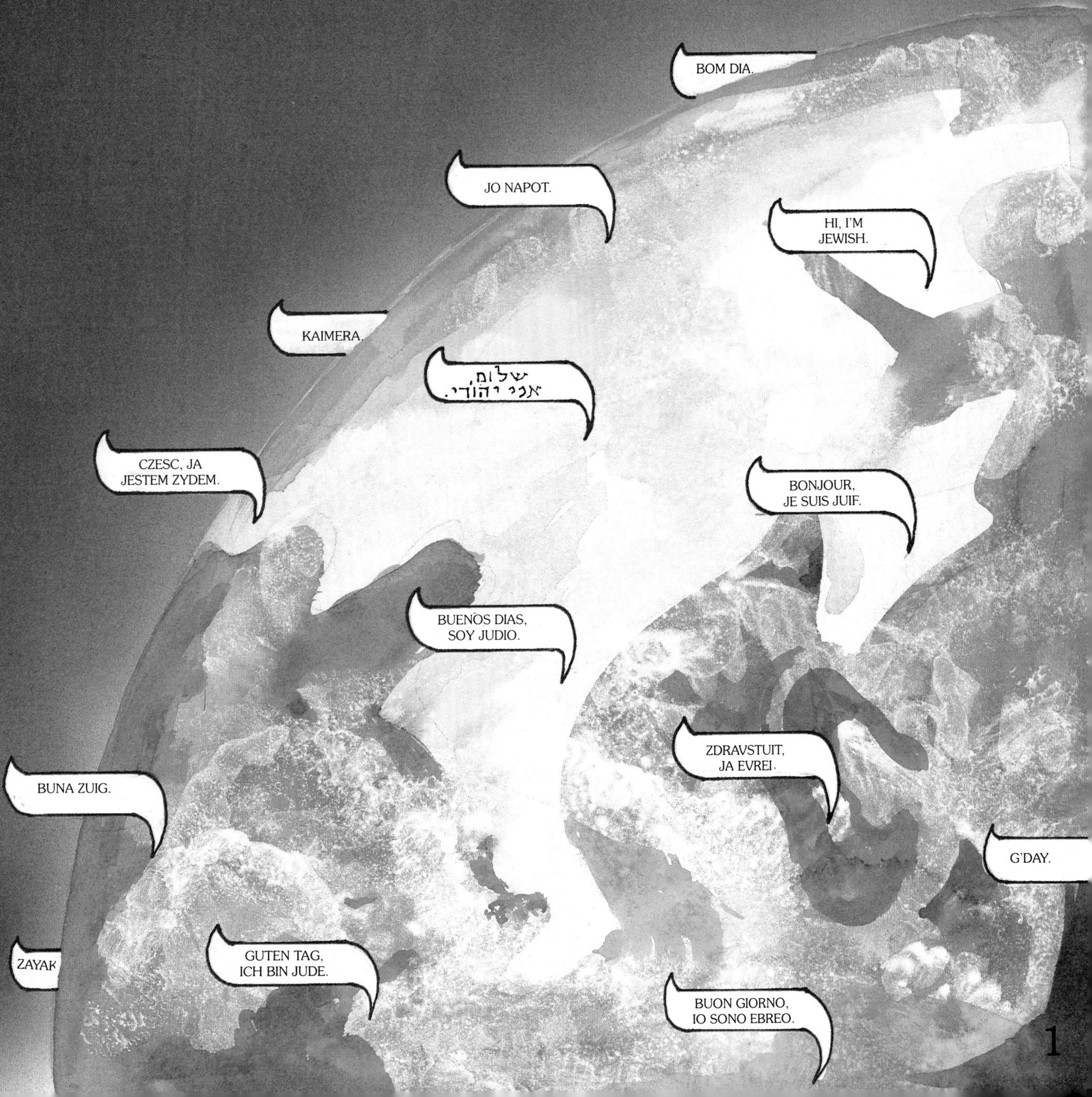

We do not look alike.
We do not dress alike.

We do not pray alike.

In Conservative and Reform congregations women read from the Torah.

A quiet prayer in Tunis

An outdoor service

Blessing the wine and ḥallah in Belgium

Some men put on tefillin when they pray in the morning on weekdays.

A hearing impaired man signs "Torah."

A congregation in Great Britain prepares to read the Torah.

But we share a belief in one God, in Torah, in Shabbat...

שלום

...and we all have synagogues.

Leningrad synagogue

Altneuschul, Prague, Czechoslovakia

Rural New England synagogue

Ramot Tziyon Congregation, Jerusalem

Ethiopian synagogue

Shaare Sholom, Kingston, Jamaica

Temple Emanu-El, Livingston, New Jersey

We all say the Shema and use Hebrew.

תורה

ברוך

חג
שמח

סידו

לשנה טובה

Braided **Ḥallah**—
Shabbat bread

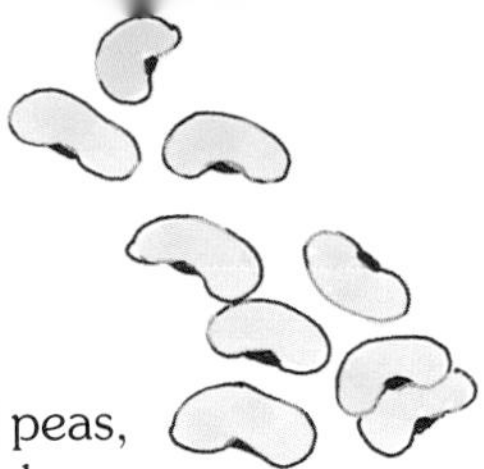

Lubiya—black-eyed peas,
Rosh Hashanah, Turkey

Blintzes—Easter
Shavuot

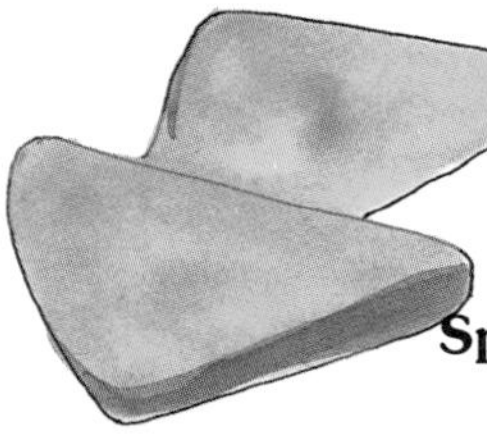

Spanakopita—Shavuot
pastry, Greece

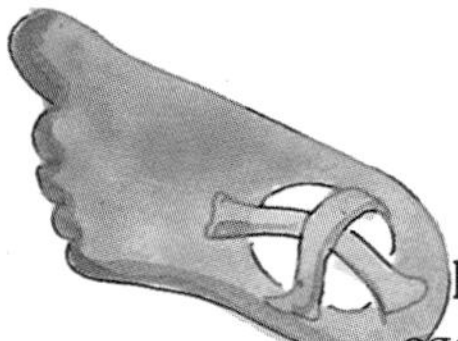

Foulares—Purim
egg and cheese pastry,
Turkey

Lemonade
preserves to

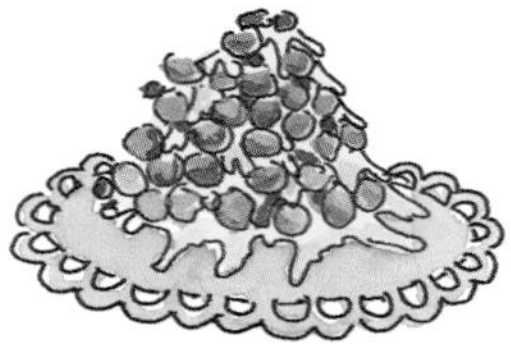

Taiglach—A
Middle-European Rosh
Hashanah treat

Ḥaroset—Pesaḥ symbol of
mortar, usually made with
fruits and nuts

Sweet Buns—
letters for break
Algeria

Potato **Latkes**—Ashkenazi
Ḥanukkah treat

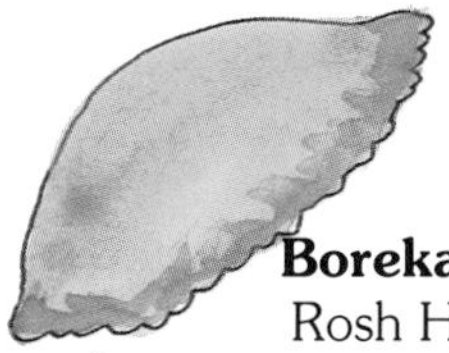

Borekas de Calabaza—
Rosh Hashanah pumpkin
turnovers, Turkey

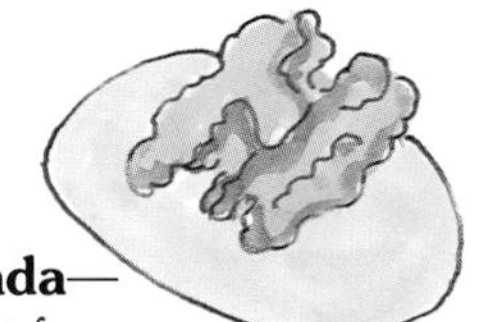

Nuez Con Almendrada—
Walnut marzipan treat for
Maimuna, Morocco

Knaidlach—Matzah balls,
Ashkenazi Pesaḥ specialty

Hamantaschen—
Ashkenazi Purim trea

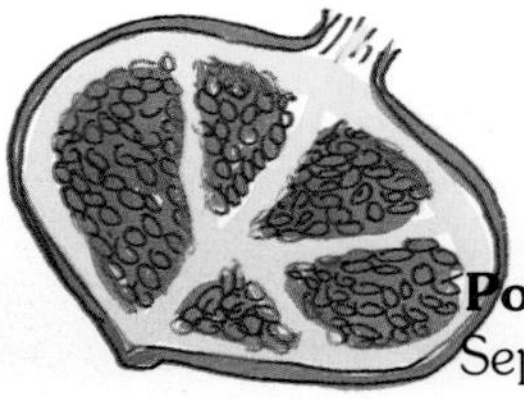

Pomegranate—Used at
Sephardi Rosh Hashanah
seder

Kra'a—Rosh Hashanah
stuffed zucchini, Syria

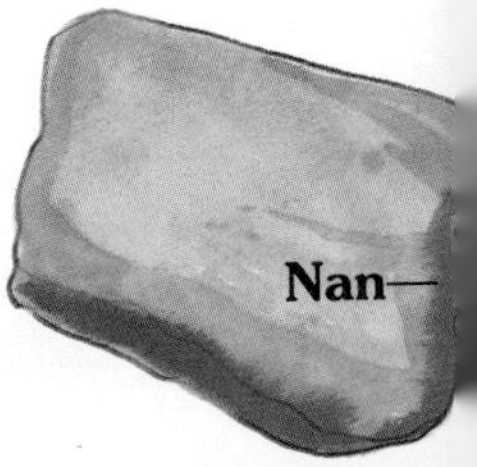

Nan—

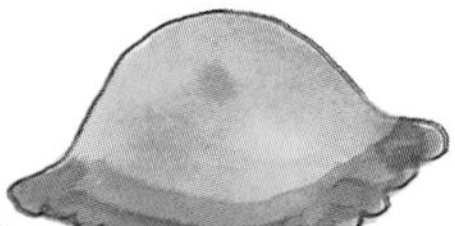

Sambusak—filled turnover,
holiday favorite, Iraq

Macaroons—Pesaḥ treat,
loved by Jews everywhere

Mogados de
Ḥanukkah sesam
Greece

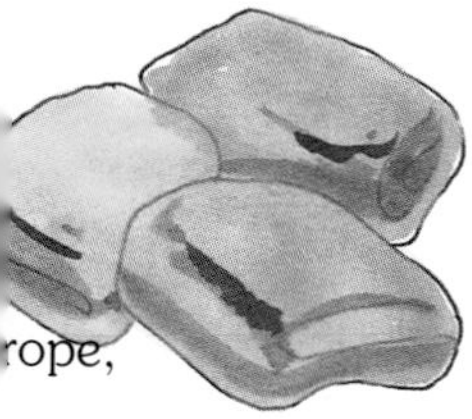

rope,

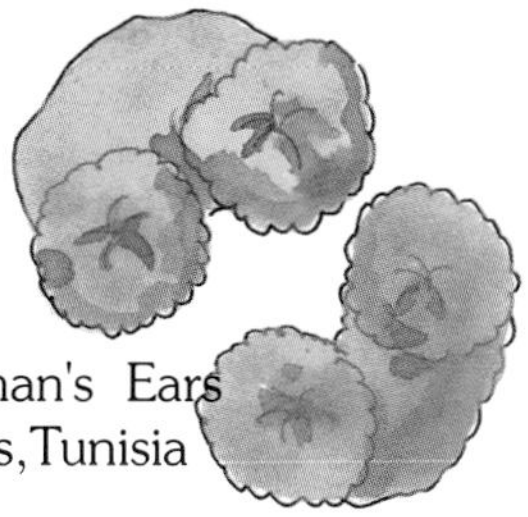

Dablah—Haman's Ears
Purim cookies, Tunisia

Herring—break-the-fast
traditional dish, Holland

Jews love to sing, dance, eat, and celebrate, especially on our Jewish holidays.

–with cherry
reak-the-fast,
ece

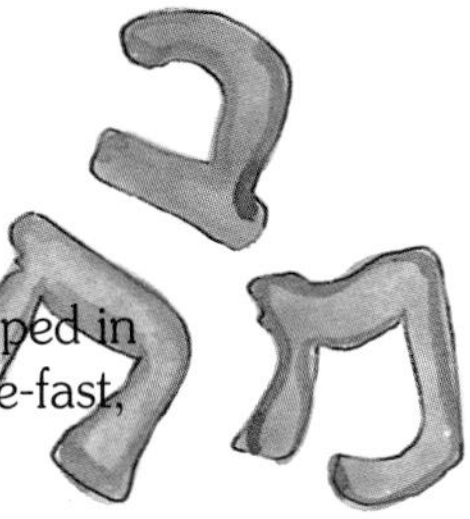

ped in
e-fast,

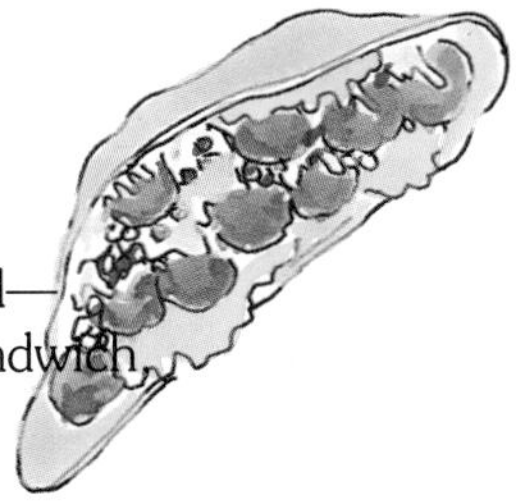

Pita with Falafel—
chickpea croquette sandwich,
Middle East

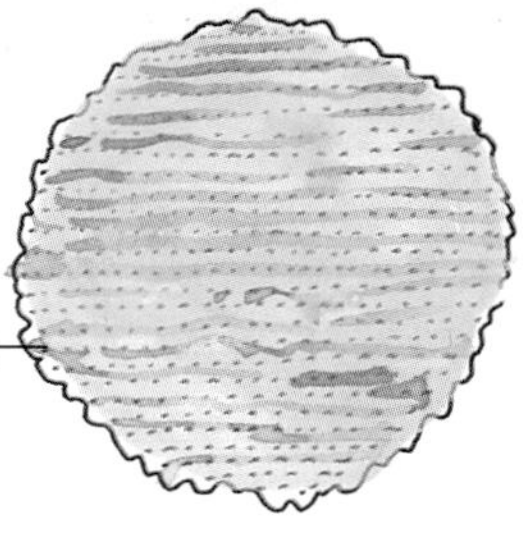

Round **Matzah**—
Sephardic

quare **Matzah**—
Ashkenazic

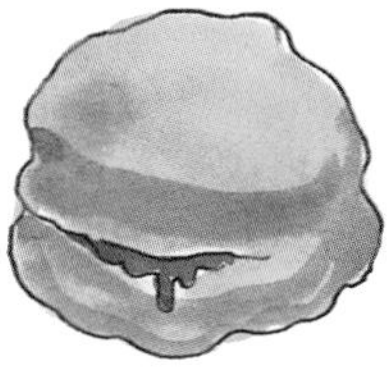

Sufganiyot—Hanukkah
donuts, Israel

Pita—Shabbat
bread, Arab countries

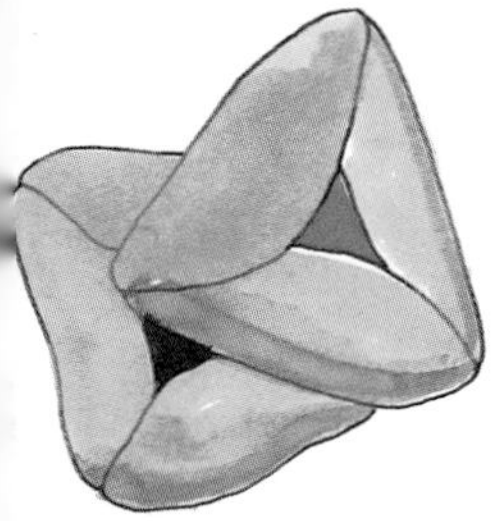

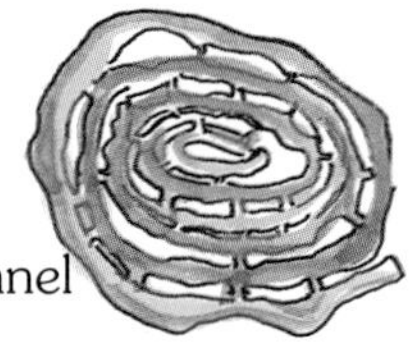

Zelabia—Purim funnel
cakes, Iraq

Hariri—Almond-milk
break-the-fast, Iraq

oliday bread, Iran
and India

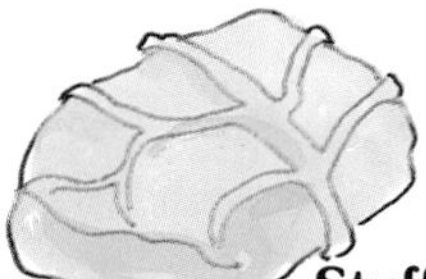

Stuffed cabbage—Sukkot
dish, Eastern Europe

Couscous—Rosh
Hashanah meal, Algeria

usam—
candies

Cholent—Ashkenazi
Shabbat dinner

Baked eggs—Sephardi
Pesaḥ seder dish

On Rosh Hashanah, we love to hear the sound of the shofar. A good New Year!

As elsewhere, children in Australia make and send Jewish New Year cards.

Man blowing the shofar in the Middle East

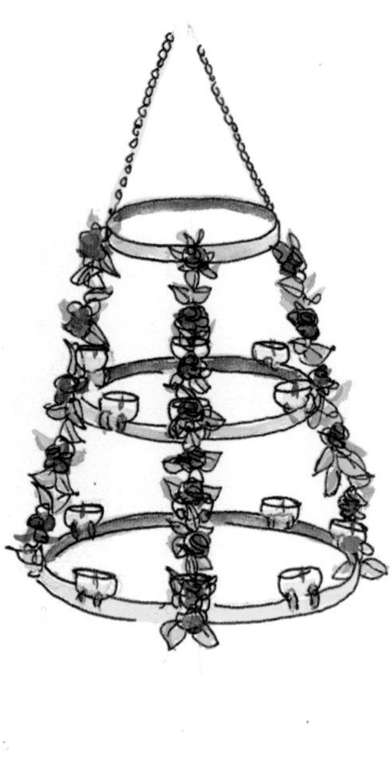

Jhumbar—an Indian New Year lamp

Hearing the shofar in the synagogue

Apples and honey for a sweet New Year

Sephardi Rosh Hashanah plate

It is a custom for many Jews to wear new clothes for the New Year.

Tashlikh—symbolically casting off sins by throwing crumbs in a body of moving water

ראש השנה
Rosh Hashanah

יום כפור

Yom Kippur

We say we are sorry to our friends if we hurt their feelings.

Yahrzeit candles are lit in memory of our relatives.

Kol Nidre is an important prayer at the beginning of the Yom Kippur Evening Service.

Many Jews dress in white.

At the end of services, Algerian children bring their fathers sweet buns shaped in their fathers' initials, to break the fast.

A blast of the shofar ends Yom Kippur services.

On Yom Kippur, we think of what we have done and what we should do. Grownups do not eat. We spend the day in synagogue.

A sukkah need have only three sides. It must be temporary. And its roof must have openings so that the sky is visible. All kinds of trees and greens are used to build a sukkah. We decorate it with fruits, vegetables, flowers, and other beautiful things.

Helping to build the sukkah

An American child brings fruits to decorate the sukkah.

סכות

Sukkot

On Sukkot, we thank God for food. We celebrate by sitting and eating in a sukkah.

A child in Cochin, India, gathers palm fronds for the sukkah.

An Israeli child gathers greens for the sukkah.

We shake the lulav (palm,myrtle, willow) and hold the etrog.

Marching in the Simḥat Torah parade

It is a custom for a Yemenite father to bring his new baby son to the synagogue for the first time on Simḥat Torah.

People gather in front of the Moscow Synagogue to celebrate.

On Simḥat Torah, we are happy because we start reading our Torah all over again.

שמחת תורה

Simḥat Torah

Grandfather leads the dancing for the first hakafah.

Sephardic Torah

Ashkenazic Torah

In Jerusalem, the Torah procession leaves the synagogue and continues through the streets of the city.

חנוכה
Ḥanukkah

A Canadian child enjoys latkes.

Syrian ḥanukkiah

Polish ḥanukkiah

Sufganiyot are a Ḥanukkah treat in Israel.

t is summer in Argentina. Children playing
lreidle have a hard time believing that when it
s Ḥanukkah in the United States it might be
snowing.

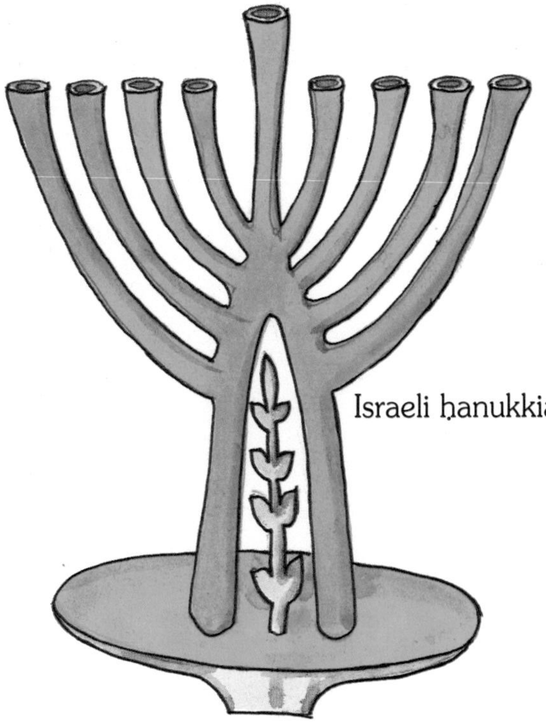

Israeli ḥanukkiah

Old stone ḥanukkiah from Yemen

A family lights the ḥanukkiah.

On Ḥanukkah, we light Ḥanukkah candles,
eat special foods, spin dreidles,
remember Judah Maccabee.

On Tu B'Shevat, we say "Happy Birthday, trees."

Some Jews have a Tu B'Shevat seder at which they eat three types of fruit—fruit with a peel, fruit with a pit, fruit which is edible inside and out. They also drink four cups of wine ranging in color from light to dark.

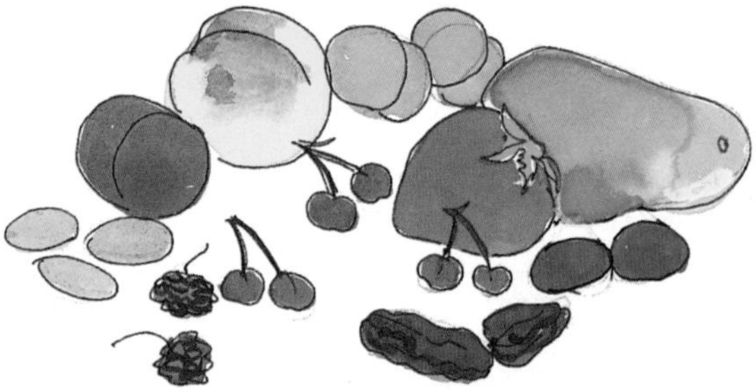

In Israel, children help plant trees.

In Venice, Italy, children feed the birds.

Along with Jews all over the world, this South African child collects money to buy trees which will be planted in Israel.

ט"ו בשבט

Tu B'Shevat

On Purim, we dress up in costumes, eat triangle-shaped foods, use noisemakers, read the Megillah, and are happy because we are free.

In South America, as elsewhere, it is a mitzvah to give money to poor people on Purim.

Iranian children help prepare bourekas, crisp pastries, for their holiday treat.

These children in Paris make so much noise when Queen Esther's story is read that no one can hear Haman's name!

Children in the United States are typical of Jewish children all over the world. They love to bring sweets and other foods, mishloah manot, to their friends and family.

Ad Lo Yada—Israelis love to watch and march in Purim parades.

A Purim spiel (play) is lots of fun for these Australian children.

פורים

Purim

פסח

Pesaḥ

The youngest child in the family sings the Ma Nishtanah, "Why is this night different from all other nights?"

Searching for ḥametz with a feather and a candle is a very old custom.

In Mexico, a boy eats matzah.

A Yemenite family enjoys its seder.

Dipping greens in salt water

In a Moroccan seder, the leader raises the seder plate over the guest's head and says "We left Egypt in a hurry."

In Ethiopia, Jews play-act leaving Egypt.

Finding the afikomen is an exciting part of the seder.

On Pesaḥ we make a seder. We eat special meals and remember that long ago Jews were slaves in Egypt.

יום השואה
Yom Hashoah

On Yom Hashoah, we remember the six million Jews who died in the Holocaust.

On Yom Ha'atzmaut, we celebrate
Israel's birthday.

Yom Ha-Atzmaut

יום העצמאות

Teenagers presenting flowers as part of the Confirmation Service, which is celebrated in Reform and some Conservative congregations when students graduate from religious school. The graduates lead the service,which often contains their own writings.

In Morocco, it is customary to throw water on passersby.

It is a tradition among Jews to eat dairy foods. This little Dutch boy enjoys cottage cheese.

שבועות

Shavuot

On Shavuot, we are happy because we were given the Torah.

In Israel, children celebrate with garlands in their hair. Baskets of fruit symbolize the harvest.

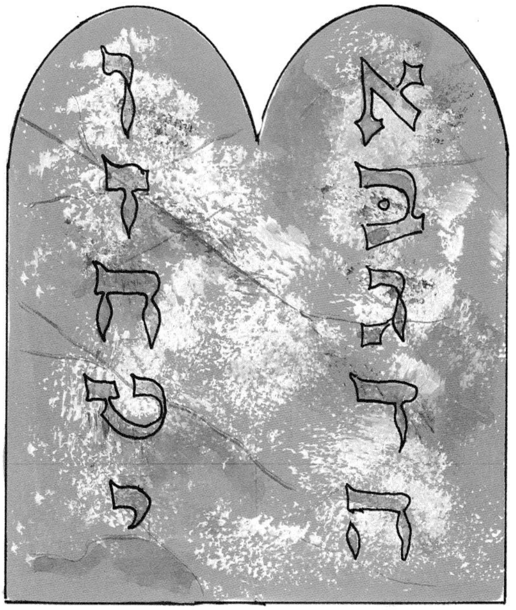

We read the Ten Commandments.

Children dance with beautiful flowers in honor of the holiday.

The rose is considered the symbol of Shavuot.

We also love to sing, dance, eat, and celebrate the important moments of our lives.

When a child is born there is a special ceremony
—a naming for a girl—a brit for a boy.

אביגיל שמשון גיטל פסח דבורה ניסים מרים

דוד דינה עקיבא מינדל שמואל ריזל

האדא מיכה רות מאיר

חיים אריאלה

גילה מתתיה הדסא

לייזר בת שבע צבי שו

זעלדא סענדר בלומה רפא

אליהו רחל שלום זיסל עמנואל

סימא יצחק שרה דניאל פרייד

שלמה ברכה אביגדור רבקה

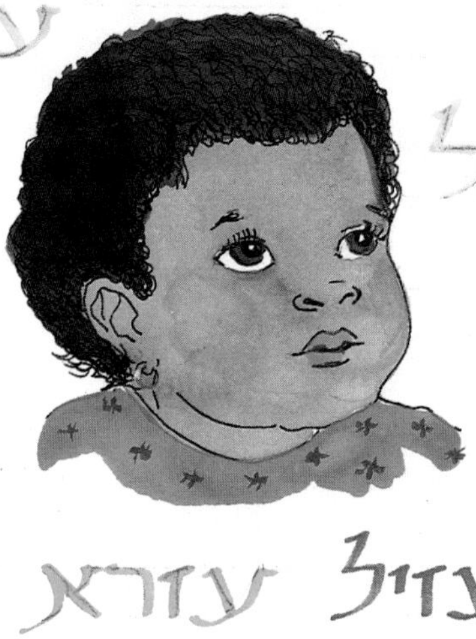

עטא יהודה מאריאשא אהרן

לפידות יאכא ישכר דרעזיל עזרא אסנת

Names are very important to Jewish people. Some children are named for living people. Some children are named in memory of people who died. But we always try to live up to our names and honor the people whose names we carry.

יקותיאל הינדא שמאי טאמארא נתן פעסיע

יוכבד טוביה ריסא יוסף עכסה אבשלום

Young children learn the aleph-bet.

Study is an important part of Jewish life.

There are few Jewish schools in the USSR. Children learn about Judaism at home.

A parent reads a Jewish book to his child.

In many places, at the start of Hebrew studies, the Rabbi prepares an aleph-bet covered with honey. The child licks the honey off all the letters.

ותלמוד תורה כנגד כלם

The parents are honored with an aliyah to the Torah at their daughter's Bat Mitzvah.

We celebrate growing up with a Bar or Bat Mitzvah, after which a Jewish child can take part in synagogue life as an adult. It is such a happy event that families eat, sing and dance to celebrate this special service.

A Bar Mitzvah in a Sephardic synagogue in Panama City

An Australian boy makes a speech at his Bar Mitzvah reception.

A Bat Mitzvah at Masada, Israel

The groom breaks the glass at the conclusion of the ceremony.

A Yemenite bride

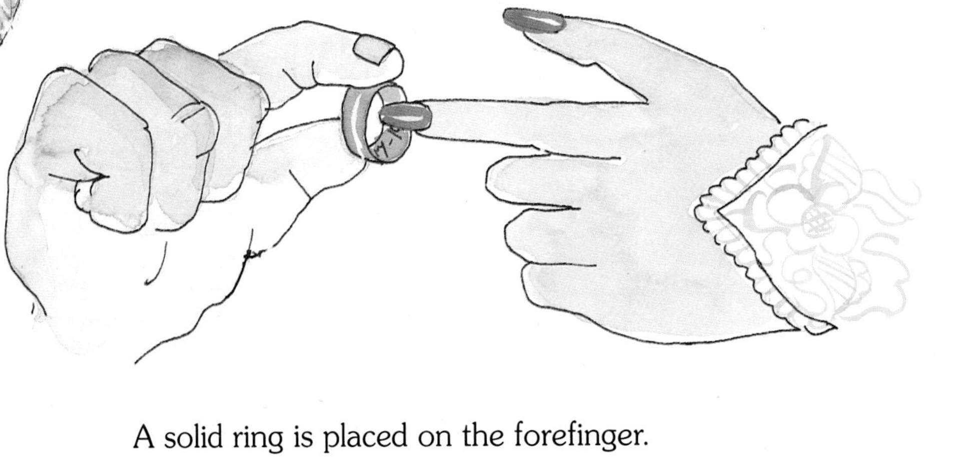

A solid ring is placed on the forefinger.

When Jews get married everyone is happy ! What a beautiful wedding! Mazal Tov!

The marriage contract, the ketubah, is read.

Wine is shared by the bride and groom.

The bride gives the groom a cone of sugar as part of the Iranian wedding ceremony.

When someone dies everyone is sad. Jews sit shiva. Friends come to offer comfort.

Jews Around the World

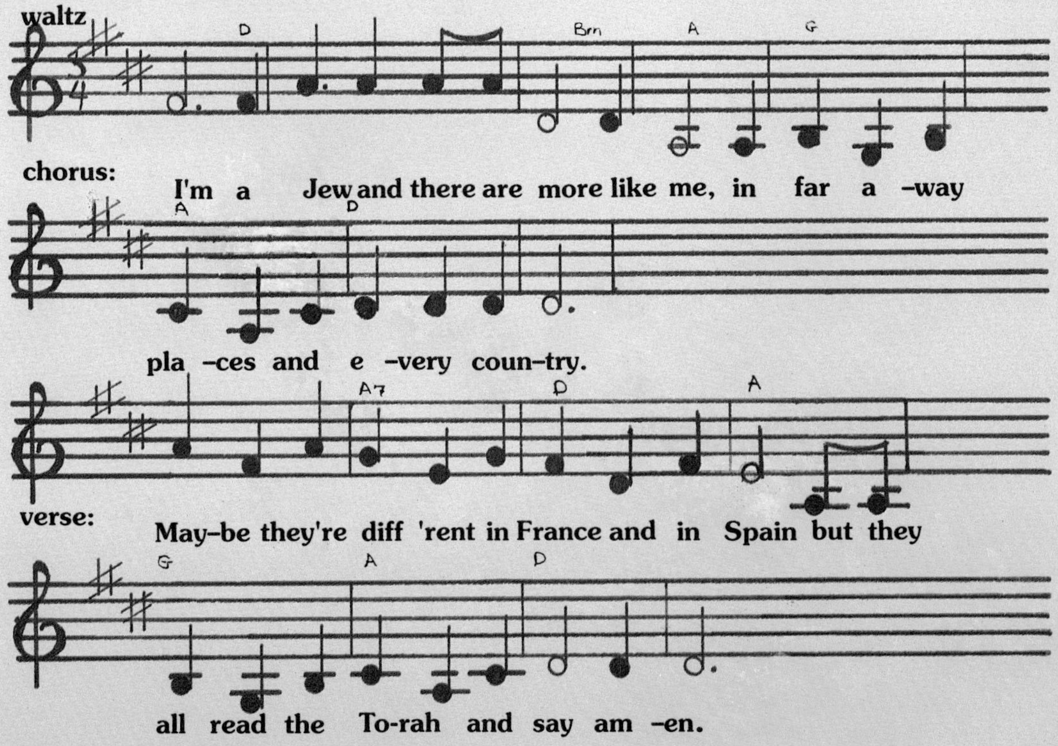

Verse 2

For many Jews
It's hard to be free
But they love to learn Hebrew
Like you and like me.

Verse 3

They talk with accents
In Scotland and Wales
But just like me, they say
Shema Yisrael.

Verse 4

Some countries are cold
And some are hot
But where Jews live
There's always Shabbat.

All Jews don't celebrate everything exactly the same way. But you can walk into any synagogue or Jewish celebration and know that you are among Jews. There are many ways to be Jewish.

L'Ḥayyim!

Glossary

Ad Lo Yada literally means "until you know nothing." It is to signify the Purim custom of drinking until you can't distinguish Haman's name from Mordecai's. It is the name of the official Purim parade held in Israel.

Afikomen from the Greek word meaning "dessert"

Aliyah literally means "going up." It is used to refer to "going up" to recite the Torah blessings on the bimah, the Torah reading platform.

Ashkenazi pertaining to Jews whose origins are eastern and central European

Bar/Bat Mitzvah a ceremony in which a thirteen-year-old is called to the Torah to celebrate becoming a member of the adult Jewish community

Break-the-Fast a meal at the end of Yom Kippur, a holy day during which adults do not eat or drink from sundown to sundown

Brit circumcision which takes place on the eighth day after birth

Etrog a citrus fruit resembling a lemon

Ḥallah a soft egg-bread

Hakafah a procession usually when the Torah is carried around the synagogue

Ḥametz food or foodstuffs which cannot be eaten or used on Pesaḥ

L'Ḥayyim "To life," often used as a toast

Maimuna a Moroccan celebration which marks the end of Passover

Mazal Tov Hebrew for "good luck"

Megillah literally means "scroll." It is most often associated with Purim. It tells the story of Queen Esther.

Mitzvah good deed and/or a commandment

Seder literally means "order." It refers to the ritual of the Pesaḥ meal.

Sephardi pertaining to Jews whose origins are in the Middle East, Asia, parts of Europe, and North Africa

Shabbat Saturday, a day of rest as prescribed in the Torah

Shema a prayer central to Judaism which translates as: "Hear O Israel, the Lord is our God, the Lord is One."

Shiva literally means "seven." The traditional length of time to observe mourning in the home.

Shofar an instrument made out of a ram's horn on which a limited number of sounds can be blown

Spiel a Yiddish word meaning "drama" or the verb "to play"

Tefillin phylacteries, leather straps connected to small boxes containing excerpts from the Torah

Torah a scroll of the Five Books of Moses

Tzedakah usually refers to the giving of money to charity

Yahrzeit Yiddish word meaning "memorial anniversary"

Acknowledgments

We wish to thank the many people who shared their family holiday and life-cycle experiences in order to make this book possible. We are especially grateful to Dr. Thomas August, Cantor Shlomo Bar-Nissim, Mr. Ernest H. De Souza, J.P., Mr. Meir Efrati, Dr. Albert Kadosh, Dr. and Mrs. Stuart Rosenthal, Dr. Gerald Ruthen, Dr. Pesach Schindler, and Mrs. Joseph Skurnik whose anecdotal descriptions and generous sharing of family and congregational photographs were invaluable in the preparation of the illustrations.